FROM COSMOS TO YOU

IT'S ALL A BEAUTIFUL POETRY RIGHT?

DEVSHISH SONAR

Made with ♥ on the Notion Press Platform
www.notionpress.com

This Book is dedicated to my family, friends, teachers and all of them who brought me knowledge and happiness.

Contents

Contents

Contents

Contents

Credits

This cover has been designed using assets from Freepik.com.

All the poems in this book were written by the poet.

The poet has self published the book.

Foreword

"Personally, i never read poems that much but this was before I saw my friend's (poet) work. I've seen him start writing them and I've seen the quality of his poems grow. Not only am I proud but I am also very impressed by his skills.

This collection of poems is by far his best work in my opinion. The poems are written in a simple way but deliver a very intellectual and deep meaning. Some of ther poems are really very sweet and all of them are immensely creative which is the best part.

The fact that this is coming from a fifteen year old baffles me. The reader would really enjoy all of the poems as many of them are very relatable and some may put a smile on their face. All in all, it will turn out to be a good experience. Kudos to the young poet for writing in such and amazing way."

-Shriya Mehendale (poet's peer)

Preface

I hope this short note finds you in a pink of health. Dear reader, I cannot be more grateful to you. Publishing this book has always been a fantasy for me. Having a lack of experience and art, I tried to convey my message as simply and beautifully as possible for my young mind. I am able to publish this book, because of YOU. I'm writing this note hoping that someone loving and lovable like you might read this.

This anthology comprises of poems originally by me. I have got experiences from my childhood, school life, animes, teachers, family, poets like John Keats, Shakespeare, Valmiki and especially- My Mother <3

My style of writing is romanticism and I've tried my best to hide a deep meaning in all the pieces. Especially the Haikus. DO NOT UNDERESTIMATE the haikus because of their small size. I've also included a poem in sanskrit so do check it out as well.

-Thank You.

1. Cosmos

Into the cosmos we wander,
to become a part of it.
Into the nebula of creation,
with red dwarves beneath.
On the rings of J1407B,
we step on the broken moons.
How unimaginable it is,
to walk on the prettiest ruins.
The supernovas attract us,
Belle and Beast together.
What are we to such great masses,
are we worth a feather?
A stellar walk is surely pretty,
within a white and black hole.
Beneath these physical and chemical reactions,
alone walks the nicest soul.

2. Oneiros

I feel an emptiness,
This isn't where I belong,
I wish to see Oneiros.
I have been waiting for so long.

Oneiros has everything.
Everything I need.
Oneiros loves me alot.
I call it mine indeed.

I seek to live there,
and forget this wrathful land.
I wish to live in Oneiros,
Oneiros is my end.

Oneiros, a city,
City of love and fantasy.
The city made of aurum,
Surrounded by milky sea.

3. Adore Her<3

Oh, Bougainville,
Shed your green leaves,
Grow pinks and whites and yellows,
Before the spring leaves.

Let the dusk shine,
On your paper flowers,
Flow with spring breeze,
Wave to hasty cars.

A lady in red sweater,
With a glamorous shine,
Passes by you in dusk,
Yes, she's the love of mine.

4. Yamasakura

Let's foster these feelings,
Let's conceal 'em all,
Let's foster our love,
Before its downfall.
I ain't an emo kid,
But I fell in love with agony,
I composed these notes and lyrics,
To form the ultimate symphony.
Oh beauty, Oh love,
Oh pink of the sakura,
Do not hide these feelings up,
Oh Yamazakura.

5. It's Only About You

Each drop for us ,
Falls from the heaven above,
To make this moment more romantic,
To strengthen the foundation of our love.
I, with my arms open wide,
Await your laughters to embrace,
You can't survive alone you know,
You're mine one and only in human race.
For whom do the buttercups bloom?
For me, the answer is you.
You're my lost self,
You're my lost shoe.
Was it destined to be this way?
Are we really meant for each other?
It seems so, on 3rd december,
When you borrow my favourite sweater.
Your lap is the best pillow,
Your arms are my only nest,
All I need is you,
Screw the rest.

6. Rainbow [haiku]

Sunlight peeps through clouds,

Its first tear reaches Earth,

Divides in seven.

7. My heaven [Sanskrit]

I don't like the heaven too if it is without you,
you're mine, oh love.
You're My Earth,
I am your Rama, Oh Sita.
My heart is small,
And you are Radha,
Your colour is great,
like roses.
I like you,
I was born for you.
You're a sunflower.
I am a busy parrot.
You are close to my heart,
Like shiva and parvati.
Our love is eternal,
Like Radha and Krishna.

मम स्वर्गम्।

त्वया विना स्वर्गमपि न रोचते,
असि मम, भो प्रिये।
त्वम असि मम पृथिवी,
अहं राम तव सिये।।

मम मनोऽस्ति सूक्ष्म:,
तव कृते मम जन्म: आसीत्।
त्वम् असि सूर्यपुष्पम्,
अहं रतशुक: किञ्चित्।।

मम मनस: समीपे त्वम् असि,
इव गिरिजाशिवौ।
नौ प्रेम: अनन्त:,
इव राधाकेशवौ।।

The original Sanskrit poem by Devshish Sonar.

8. Feelings [Haiku]

Feelings can't be said,

Like the pain a dear bears,

Speechless and alone.

9. Boundless Words[Haiku]

Words slip through the tongue,

Like a dove boundless and free

Shall one hold it tight?

10. Nothing Is Forever[Haiku]

Nothing's forever,

We shall seperate as well,

Time's not forever.

11. Faded Rainbows[Haiku]

Rainbows fade as well,

There is nothing one can tell,

For you though I fell.

12. Bubblegum [Haiku]

Bubblegum you are,

Very sweet and very sour,

My buttercup sweet.

13. Miserable Life[Haiku]

Miserable life,

Do your work and go kiss death,

Life is too unfair.

14. Christmas Eve

A gift with a bow,
A tree in the snow,
Red dress for my niece,
And cold winter breeze.
A lovely holiday,
With a man bearded grey,
Jumping down the chimney,
For milk and a cookie.
Rudolph with a jingle bell,
Plum cakes on the sell,
Woolen clothes around,
Snowflakes on the ground.
Shovels in the yard,
A starbucks voucher card,
A kid with a gift to buy,
2 truths and a lie.

15. Under The Umbrella

Walking with wet shoes,
Under the white umbrella,
There is a place for two,
that shall be filled by you, Cinderella.

The beats of these drops,
Remind me of you, oh maiden,
Nobody can bring sun in my life,
You are the only one.

My heart seems to sink,
in the burdens bestowed by life,
Will you like to be my sunshine?
Would you like to be my wife.

16. Crow[Haiku]

Scared of golden straws,

Black follows death and mourning,

Beauty in itself.

17. Fjord[haiku]

Oceans strecthes arms ,

Spreads its smell through some valleys,

A norwegian fjord.

18. Dead End

The agony, the sorrow,
the despair and grief.
I wish that sooner fell,
My life's last leaf.
Speechless and depressed,
I merely live lifeless,
I wanna feel that cremation,
I wanna live life less.
I've had it all,
I've seen my part,
All that is left is,
Life's last art.
I don't wanna burden,
Or be one either,
I wanna fly,
but I lack a feather.

19. My Star

They blabber alot,
You're not my type they say,
They show me dreams of the green grass,
But what attracts me is the golden hay.
Love has never been a piece of cake,
but you're making it my cup of tea.
Thanks for bringing me the roses,
Thanks for falling in love with me.
I have a phobia of love,
but am a philophile.
What makes me fall in love with love,
is that cute and silly smile.
Be open to me and say it all,
I love the way you are,
No way Europa is prettier,
Than my luminous star.

20. Garden of Love

Our garden of love,
please shine on it.
I spent my tears,
to water it.
Please embrace me,
and hold me close.
Give me my daily,
Anti-depressant dose.
Don't hurt me please,
I love you the most.
You are a sea arc,
On my rocky coast.
We are halves,
of heart of Aphrodite,
Please hurry towards me,
with unprescedented might.

21. Even if a bit...

Only if I could help,
Even if a bit.
I wanna strangle threads,
The bonds I wanna knit.
I know i ain't a priority,
But even if a choice,
Even if all I get is a while,
I do wish to rejoice.
Everything 'bout you is a gift,
Including the ignorance,
I wish to convey it all,
All I await is a chance.
You may ditch me for better,
The ones you love more,
But we both do know,
It was never a chore.

22. Wish for me in Agartha

The day I become a memory,
Will you wish for me in Agartha?
Will you be my Savitri?
This is why we exist, Yeah?
The human feelings too pale,
To describe this bond of infinity,
Pretending hate hurts more,
we don't hold no enmity.
The Satan will too desire,
This love of ours so strong,
I can't hate you. Never.
Please don't get me wrong.
You are my gift of Magi,
Maybe you are Pandora,
You have all my answers,
You indeed are my Quora.

23. Eschaton

During Eschaton,
Will you look for me?
Will you try to see me?
Will you shed tears in the search?
Will the world erupt
while I am in your arms?
Will the Gods forgive us for our love?
For our lust and desires?
For our emotions?
For you?
For me?
Will the doomsday be a date?
Will it be our end too?
Will you come to hell to look for me?
Or will you enjoy alone in paradise?
Will you befriend the angels or will you leave them for me?
Will you be alright with me working for Lucifer?
Will we be the same afterlife?
Or will the Gods object?

24. FUSEN

Her love tastes like fusen,
sweet, pink and sour.
However hard you may stretch it,
it is yet ours.
I chew on it till the taste lasts,
and pop the bubble of curiosity,
and walk along the dim paths
of the nights of this sleepless city.
Japanese love you have darling,
pink like sakura and cold like snow.
Imported and expensive your love is,
It makes me broke you know.
It is addictive oolala,
gets me high everytime,
your love tastes like Fusen,
your love is a beautiful rhyme.

25. Nemesis

The ambivalence is sadistically joyful,
for you though, not me.
Did we have to let go?
Gracias for setting me free.
Conquered by thee I want to be,
but freedom is a necessity.
It's not JUST joy and relief,
It's also sorrow, loneliness and pity.
We did become our downfall,
you abducted my love and fate.
Even though it ended bad,
why do I see no hate?

26. I love how you never give up...

The values when we were young,
we lose them as we grow.
But you never let 'em go,
The reason is what I wanna know.
The world it wants me to give up,
But you yet stannd like a buttercup,
You are leading us all to truth,
You want the world to wake up.
You pray to the Gods above,
I see you in shrines till now,
Even with the prayers unanswered,
You never break apart somehow.
I wonder if Gods exist,
or are they just ignoring us?
I love how you visit temples,
and never miss the tuesday morning bus.
Yet your bold unshhok courage,
will make your prayers reach up.
That is what I love about you,
I love how you never give up.

27. Catacombs [haiku]

Peaceful death lies here,
Under the city of love,
a nice attraction.

28. Rose's Red

The words to my poems,
I do know I write them,
but they flow through your love,
you cause this mayhem.

You are the nature,
You are its beauty,
Stop swimming now, will you?
We have already reached the shore of the sea.

Everything is great over here,
except girls, there is no you,
You are mt rose's red,
You are my Violet's blue. <3

29. Waterfall [haiku]

Pretty mass suicide,
Droplets fall from the mountain,
Along with salmons.

30. Iceberg [haiku]

Some ice peeks above,
Most of it covered with lies,
Hazardous white land.

31. Taj mahal [haiku]

Death also loves love,
They live in the same white stone,
A wonder of world.

32. Seeking Joy

Why do our hands move before we think?
Relationships rupture in franctions of blink.
The frost grows on frozen snow,
People go and leave sorrow.
We seek happiness in life's luxury,
But leave shunned true joy's sea.
We seek happiness in an unaffordable tuxedo,
But forget to find it in the way we grow.
Suicidal thoughts may seek you,
It isn't a storm but a dew.
Turning into mist it will fade,
Sunshine of peace will find your way.
Buddies and blood are there for you,
Halley's comet in a dark sky blue.
Life is a never ending game,
Made for those who can stay tame.

33. The Peace of the Sun

Every night the same dream,
Every day the same nightmare.
How did I turn into this?
Did I lose myself where?
Cutting bonds with people who love,
For forgiving those who don't.
I have undergone few changes,
but i swear anymore I won't.
I just want to find peace,
In whatever form I may get.
But it was just finding the sun,
hours after the sunset.
You know that it exists,
but you can never look at it.
I realised it too late,
with me the bright suns sit.

34. Dead End

The agony, the sorrow,
despair and grief.
I wish that sooner fell,
mty life's last leaf.
Speechless and depressed,
I merely live lifeless,
I wanna feel that cremation,
i wanna live life less.
I have had it all,
I have seen my part,
All that is left is,
life's last art.
I don't wanna burden,
or be one either,,
i wanna fly,
but lack a feather.

35. Where your beauty lives [haiku]

There lies my poor soul,
Where your beauty lives as well,
but walls block our route.

36. Us in sunset [haiku]

Will you ever come?
Stay with me till the sunset.
Till the rays don't leave.

37. Love me [haiku]

Love me like you did,
Love me forever sweetheart,
Love me till we die.

38. Lonely sans you [haiku]

Lonely I have been,
sans your love and care and you,
when will the gaps fill?

39. I Love You to the Moon and Back

I love you till the moon and back,
can I be your evening snack?
Yes, I am the owner of those arms of yours,
Babyy, I live for you, of course.
Not talking to you is like skipping sleep,
withou you I alone at night weep.
I do love you, I do, alot.
Just trynna play my game smart.
I have seen heartbreaks, it broke me down,
But you are the best in town.
Oh Europa, let me in your heart.
Let me love you my part.

40. For Us<3

All the sea I see today,
'morrow will turn to mist,
the bodies that wander Earth,
will become ashes in a fist.
Why are we having hope?
We know that the life will end,
Is it a beauty of life?
Or is it God's command?
If it was to slip out of my hand,
Why was it ever given to me?
WE exist in the only fear,
if we get tomorrow to see.
Maybe it had to be this way,
Maybe it is so for us,
MAybe it was for this love,
It definitely was for us.

41. I Love You just the Way I Do

They say the moon will turn to rings,
If it comes close to embrace Earth.
Be my moon honey; get that close,
let your ring embrace my hand.
Let our love be maple,
shed your tears like trees shed leaves,
fall for me like those leaves,
fly with me like those seeds.
You've always been a sakura on Fuji,
hiding love, hate, feelings and truths,
but when they reveal, it feels like spring,
Knowing you is always comforting.
You are aurora, too complex to know,
Yet shine the way you do,
a glance too feels heavenly,
That is why I love you the way I do.

42. A Possessive Sweetheart

Being possessive I swear,
no guy shall ever lay a hand on you again,
if he does, he dies,
he gets to see the literal heaven.
I feel jealousy when they do,
I cry silent tears,
but how would you ever know
with those deaf ears?
I love you alot don't I?
Can't I be possessive too?
I don't want anything,
All I want is you.
I am sorry for being the way I am,
but nobody shall ever touch,
my darling too sweet and kind,
I love you that much.

43. End of me

I see the end of me,
not too far from me,
an end of sorrow and sufferings,
an end without thee.
I see my blood flowing,
or me hanging on the fan,
in my 'good dreams' I'd say,
In which rest in peace I can.
I see my best friends cry,
on my funeral's mourning day,
I see smiles on few faces,
the people ho betray.
Not much worth I have,
to have a great exit,
to hide my murder they
hid me in a pit.

44. Naturing with Nature

The wind brings me joy,
with some salty smell of fjord.
The rivers bring me blessings,
nestowed by Mountain God.
The flowers bow to sun,
to respect its majesty.
The moss finds a way to grow,
on a path unused dusty.
The gravity of nature attracts me,
never lets my attention soar.
The nature is an eternal teacher,
who always teaches more.

45. Worthy of smile [haiku]

Why you wish to smile?
Are you worthy of smiling?
Maybe maybe not.

46. Lovely People [haiku]

Everyday's same,
But you've got lovely people,
To make life better <3

47. Living trash [haiku]

you are living trash,
but maybe useful to them,
a reason living.

48. Their Side [Haiku]

you merely live,
for their happiness and peace,
never leave their side.

49. Your Name [Haiku]

god's blessing's your name,
let name be a character,
be miraculous.

50. Summer 2022

Heat wves melting the air,
yellow flames on trees,
soda pops in the shops,
Warm dusty breeze.

Spending time writing,
with the sunlight like a lightning,
burning down everything,
dominating my thinking.

Pride of India with purples,
Yellow flames with birds,
kids locked in homes,
and busy working nerds.

The cola so tempting,
but my pocket empty broke.
Drinking water and back to work,
dreaming to buy the coke.

51. Reign of Darkness[haiku]

Darkness spreads its wings,
Will one with light save us here,
Will luck shine on us.

52. Loyalty dies

I never saw any care,
alone my dead love cries.
Thanks for making me realise,
even loyalty dies.
I always wondered if,
you were really my astronaut?
But when I found the true ones,
I understood you were not.
I thought I saw my future in you.
Those were merely my desires.
All the heavens of love and care,
are now burning with wrathful fires.
It is better if you disappeared,
I am ready for a closure.
We kept drifting farther away,
In the process of getting closer.

53. The People Who Die

The people who die,
Don't they deserve to smile more?
Do we smile up there?
Is there any 'up' for sure?
The people who die,
do they live the afterlife?
Do they think, feel or do?
Is there anything after life?
The people who live,
yet worry on inanimate things.
They mourn over personal beliefs,
and not accept what fate brings.
Is this world so awful,
we wish to die to find joy?
Is this world so immature,
there will always be a fall of Troy?

54. The Twilight We See

The magical hour it is,
during the twilight pink.
Watching the nights fall,
my heart starts to sink.
Will this night be treacherous?
and test my endurance?
Will it bring a brighter morn'?
One that never ends?
Though pretty the twilight is,
a contemporary reality...
Every child shall enjoy the present,
provided with clarity.
Purple floof I see in sky.
The wealthy might be seeing it too.
Money seems to change nothing,
few things are always true

55. New Years

Where is the 'new' of new years?
Melancholy and sorrow repeat.
Unwillingly and unknowingly,
millions of old hearts beat.
Happy and new are desires,
that remain unfulfilled.
These happy and new desires,
Every new year killed.
Is this reality just a halluscination?
Are we where we were meant to be?
Are we really alive?
Is it true what we see?

56. The Day We Met

The day we met,
was it really a coincidence?
but you really got me, you know,
we never lost touch,hence.
I know things had changed.
We were soon into dating.
Near the blossoms in the park,
you kept me waiting.
We had to break up too,
we were twenty years old.
Running after jobs and gigs,
for money we were sold.
Today, i am forty,
you living in my house.
From lovers we advanced.
Thanks for staying, my spouse.

57. Falling from Lhotse

Falling from Lhotse,
Falling for you.
My eyes are wet and soaked,
bawling for you.
You kill me from the inside,
you puncture my heart.
You broke my emotions into pieces.
You feast on its each part.
You make me fall in love with you.
You are what I desire.
Your promises aren't trustworthy.
You're a bloody liar.
I want you so bad I'd die.
Die for your love and all I care.
I only want you with me.
Only some time to spare.

58. Morning Grapefruit [haiku]

Then the sun shines high,

Grapefruit high in the mighty sky.

Beginnings begin.

59. Dew[haiku]

The dews then gather,
grass holding small waterfalls,
relaxes my feet.

60. Cloudy game [haiku]

Then comes the white moon,
Shining up gloriously,
Hide and seek with clouds.

61. Wolf [haiku]

And the midnight falls,
Howls a hound breaking silence,
Asleep the town is.

62. Homemade Chocolate

The sweet cranberries,
As sweet as your voice,
saved from the bugs and pests,
the pests like your boys.
Getting your hands messy,
You prepare the homemade chocolate.
Your sweet and love is what
makes me wanna wait.
The taste so delightful,
the artist though more.
As sweet and special
as my heart's core.

63. Girlfriend to Pen friend

These fictional knives poke me through,
yet here I am trynna convey.
Even if you're not there to listen,
maybe this is my way.
I remember how you had me whole,
but all I see now is a silhouette.
I wish the time unfolded and mended,
and returned to the day we met.
Maybe tolerance is all I have,
maybe this is what keeps us together.
Maybe I wasn't satisfactory,
That is why you left for better.
I won't say we don't talk,
but our coversations end.
The transformation did hurt me,
from Girlfriend to pen friend.

64. Value of My Tears.

Do my tears have any value?
In front of those diamond drops.
You saw them and left me,
and hurt me till my tear pops
Am I that unlovable?
Am I that unworthy?
That you left me for the people,
who are as fake as one can be.
I wonder if I meant anything
to you or your ferric heart.
I wonder, just wonder,
wonder till the very start.

65. I didn't Realise You

I should have loved you more,
for you are sweet and nice.
You always stood alongside,
like Onigiri's rice.
You are small and sour,
you are gifted with a scar.
Even though you are afar,
you are actually a star.
You are cosmology.
You are astrology.
You are my psychology.
You are my life's chronology.
I love you my pal.
You are prettier than the Sun.
Shine in the vacuum and dark matter,
smile on a long run<3

66. Hug him before He Leaves

He will be there,
always.
But make sure he lasts,
death isn't under his control.
He seeks his love in you,
for he is weak, very weak.
He is inches away from his death,
just inches.
He gets hurt everytime,
clinging to hangman's knot.
Oh knot, please break or kill.
Either ways , he will be free again.
He may leave soon,
so hug him.
Show him he belongs to you,
so he won't leave.

67. Vortex

Let's swirl into a vortex,
the shape of everything.
The figure of birth and death.
A song that universes sing.
The galaxies like Andromeda,
and devotee flowers of Sun,
follow a definite path,
a beautiful vortex to run.
Vortices decide existence.
Vortices rule destruction.
Vortices control gravitation.
Vortices boost creation.
The whirlpools of masses
unite in a vortex.
Vortices decide all.
Vortices are our index.

68. Meaningless Love

Nothing ever had a meaning.
Was it all pretend fake?
How did my little gecko
turn into this deadly snake.
Am I halluscinating?
I wish to see you in my dreams.
I feel like avoiding you in reality,
are you just an imagination? It seems.
The dragons of the clouds,
and the mighty Chimera.
now I know why disappeared,
it's because of this fake love's era.
I've started hating poetry.
Self loathing is my new interest.
I only see problems,
while searching for rest.

69. Thirst {haiku}

Thirst kills me inside,
Shall a drop wet my dry throat?
I am desperate.

70. Let Me...

Since I saw you that day,
You won't ever be unseen.
Your elegance caught these eyes of mine,
let's fill the gaps in between.
let's walk our hearts to finish line,
the line that lies at my tomb.
Let us occupy the same residence,
let my child occupy your womb.
I know this sounds too cheesy,
I'm ok being cringe for you.
Let the neighbours envy us,
let them know love can be true.
Let me cook a meal for you,
after we have a silly fight.
Let me turn the lamps off for you,
let me kiss you a good night.

71. Waiting For Spring [haiku]

Will pink blossoms fall?
Will the lake fly in the sky?
Will thirst kill me too?

72. Summer Flowers [haiku]

Pride of India,
Spread purples in this town dull,
Paint the summer day.

73. My Summer Popsicle[haiku]

Yellow flames on trees,
Twirl down with blowing hot winds.
My popsicle melts.

74. Waiting for Winds [haiku]

I wait for thou winds,
Bring a drop of life with thou winds,
bring oceans with thou.

75. Globe ablaze [haiku]

The globe set ablaze.
My heart melts with burning sun.
Hot cold the day is.

76. A Weird Proposal

Lend me your soul.
Your heart is my goal.
Losing you does gnaw,
and leaves me with your awe.
I hate to say it but I have to.
I am desperate for you.
I know that this might not seem true.
But your eyes are deep like ocean blue.
I hope we share this affection.
Having you besides provides satisfaction.
I chase you like a strong attraction.
My life's been broken into fractions.
The hourglass with the falling sand
reminds me to hold on to your hand
before we reach till the tail end.
Would you accept me as your boyfriend?

77. Starfish and Dolphin

The starfish that clinged to the dolphin,
fell and got lost on the seabed.
The sand, swordfish, sharks and tuna,
is all the starfish had.
The swordfish slices through.
The sharks feed on sliced parts.
The salty sand then ignites the wounds.
The tuna, a prey itself, rips it apart.
The oceanic currents shall set it free.
Why won't the dolphin return?
Did it find its mammal pod?
Is the dolphin having fun?

78. Last moments

Hold my hands before they shatter,
I see them digging my grave.
Let this life be rescued by you,
the only one who can save.
Spread your arms and hug me tight,
and never let me go.
Kiss my lips and tell me 'I love you',
just to let me know.
All we have is now to live,
I see your future without me,
a future gloomy agonizing,
a future we don't want to see.
I ain't here forever,
every guy breathes his last.
You know it's only sorrow,
time flies fast.

79. Vanilla Bean

As you walk in the corridor,
ignoring you is a sin.
Just as sweet and fragrant you are,
My french Vanilla Bean.
You tiptoe on the staircase,
I fear you might fall.
I call for you loud and clear,
when I don't even want to call.
You attract me and disappear.
Oh my! You're so mean.
Just stay with me forever please,
my french vanilla bean.

80. Spring, it's here.

The crickets singing a symphony.
The yellow shrug of trees.
The Bougainville dancing,
and the sweet odour of breeze.
The birds chirping along,
vocalising to sing a song.
It's a harmony, an unplanned harmony,
with a sky that has never been so sunny.
The petals on the roads,
not even a single cloud in the magnificent sky.
The butterflies flying carelessly,
waving the winters a goodbye.
The season that brings life,
and a beautiful song to hear.
Everything around tells me,
'Spring it's here.'

81. Left me alone?

Looking at you I cry,
why did you have to die?
It should have been me.
Why helpless do I lie?
Can we go back to those days,
where the little you stays.
'I will stay forever'
where the little you says.
Can I hug you for once again?
Your memories drive me insane.
My sanity is struggling to defeat,
this agonizing solitude's pain.
I can see you again when,
I wanna skip time to then.
I can bring the sky down,
to see you in heaven.
Don't I deserve the sweet kiss
which brought to me heavenly bliss?
Those days, the golden ones,
are the ones that I miss.

82. I am All Yours

My heart conveys its love for you,
with every light pulse.
You ignite these flams inside of me,
with your flawless inflammables.
You flow in my veins,
I breathe you in with air.
You invade my dreams without permit.
My girl you're unfair.
My arms want to be your home.
My laps shall be your sofa.
My grave shall be your's neighbour,
yes, i do dream of so far.
My chest shall be your pillow,
hear my heart beat before you sleep.
Let my t shirt be your towel,
to wipe your dew drops tears while you weep.

83. Questions

The questions I ask,
innocent, curious, but tricky,
do make you get entangled.
Your answers, for sure are picky.
I love how you answer,
leaving me confused.
You are the reason for these doubts,
you are the one accused.
Though I love the way it is,
I wish for it to be the same.
I know it hurts, I know it does,
yet let us continue this love's game.

84. Monsoon

The dream catcher jingles,
the winds bring a letter.
Right on our threshold,
is the rainy weather.
The warm cup of coffee,
the howling sound of air.
Daughter looking for her brother,
the son hiding under the chair.
Me and their mother on the couch,
watching WandaVision.
Ever moving on from this?
I have got no reason.
A day off from work,
a day with family,
though my pay will be reduced,
I will enjoy this happily.

85. Speechless sweet calls.

I call you and you pick,
you break the ice with a 'hi'.
And then we are speechless,
leaving each other on standby.
Taking my heart in hands,
getting my BP high.
I try to make an excuse,
"I can't hear you, why?"
We go quite and numb again,
and the winter snowflake falls.
I fall in love with these
speechless sweet calls.

86. Library

The silence of the noises,
written in the books.
Inside the shelves of worlds,
a young reader looks.

Is there something to worry us?
I don't think there is.
Just the books and me
and the eternal bliss.

The love, the revenge,
the stories on these pages.
The knowledge all collected,
contracted from the ages.

The heavenly loneliness,
the one that I desire.
The only solitude needed,
the only solitude I admire.

87. An Alternative Sweetheart.

Am I just an alternative,
for the world so much fun?
Am I just an alternative,
like a king's third son.
I thought I meant something,
somebody to you darling.
Seems I wasn't. Never.
I never had any meaning.
My existence means nothing.
I am just a replacement.
If it was gonna slip away,
why was it ever sent?
I guess you found the better,
I may too one day.
To me, you are always the best,
what else do I have to say?

88. Your Way of Keyboard

The way you press the keys,
the way it rings everytime.
The way I visualise petals,
whirling down in frozen time.
The way you let it ring,
the way your silence rhymes.
The way it lets hues spread,
reds, blues and limes.
The way your emotions flow,
the happiness and sorrow.
It surely reaches me,
because I love how you play the key.

89. Where Your Breath Flows

When I laughed besides you,
it felt like time froze.
I just want to stay there,
where your breath flows.
It smells like fresh Canele,
just taken out of the warm oven.
I only want to make memories,
the sweet and special ones.
The wind that touches your shoulder,
smells like the wind of lavendar farms.
The only place that feels cozy,
are your cozy arms.
I just want to stay there,
where this fragrant wind blows.
I just want to stay there,
where your breath flows.

90. You

My morning, my sunshine.
A sunkissed picture of perfection.
My beauty, my joy.
Physical form of my affection.
Your smile as bright as summers,
your touch as cold as ice.
Your words are sweet like pastries,
also as hot as spice.
Your hair flows with winds,
Your hair, the black Tocantins.
Your words paint the cosmos,
your words, a koi's fins.
How do I ever leave you?
The value of your 'g' is highest.
You mean everything to me,
everything at its best.

(PS: g here refers to accelaration due to gravity in scientific terms)

A Letter For You

The room that feels like home,

The land where you are loved,

The city which is your dreams.

2 February, 2023.

Dear ____________________________,

I hope this letter finds you in a pink of health. I hope this letter finds you in a state of joy. The fact that you are reading this letter makes me feel happy and loved. This letter was meant for you to read someday. To bring you joy. To bring you happiness. To express my love for you.

You are beautiful. You matter. I am very proud of you for living all those years, months, weeks, days, hours, minutes, seconds and moments. Just existing in this world requires a lot of luck and courage. There are infinite galaxies in our observable universe. Each galaxy exists with billions of stars, supernova, nebula and black holes. Each star has its own stellar system. Each stellar system has those moons, aesteroids, planets, comets and celestial bodies. Out of these infinite possibilities, you took birth on the only planet confirmed to have life on it. Even this planet has many species. You could have been a dinosaur and have died a tragic death. You could have been the ant you stepped on unknowingly. You could have been the dog who passed away few days ago and you saw it on social media. But no, you were born as you. You could have been born in the timeline where people died of black death. People died of spanish flu, AIDS but you didn't. You were born in a timeline when you could live easily and safely. There are millions of books out there yet you brought this book and read this letter. That's how special you are <3

Never feel down. Never ever disgrace yourself. You are loved. You are worthy. Never give up. Never ever.

Yours lovingly,

Devshish Sonar.

criticalboy777@gmail.com

9 798889 597636

Printed by Libri Plureos GmbH in Hamburg, Germany